Eve

19__

The Top News Stories of the Year

By Hugh Morrison

Montpelier Publishing
London

ISBN-13: 978-1545460221
ISBN-10: 1545460221
Published by Montpelier Publishing, London.
Printed and distributed by Amazon Createspace.
This edition © 2017. All rights reserved.

Events of
1967

'I can't see anything!'

Campbell's world water speed attempt ends in tragedy

Donald Campbell (inset) attempting the world water speed record in *Bluebird K7*, moments before the craft overturned.

Donald Campbell CBE was an experienced racing driver who had previously set the world land speed record of 440 mph in the *Bluebird CN7* car in Australia.

On 4 January 1967 he attempted to break the world water speed record on Coniston Water in England's Lake District in his experimental boat, *Bluebird K7*

Designed by Ken and Lew Norris, the *K7* was a steel framed, aluminium bodied, three-point hydroplane with a Metropolitan-Vickers Beryl axial-flow turbojet engine, producing 3,500 pound-force (16 kN) of thrust. Although reaching a peak speed of 328mph on part of the course the craft began to behave erratically and eventually somersaulted, breaking on impact and sinking before help could arrive.

His last words over the intercom were 'I can't see anything...I've got the bows out...I'm going...' Despite extensive searches, Campbell's body and the wreckage of *Bluebird K7* were not recovered until May 2001.

'Boston Strangler' escapes from jail

Notorious serial killer on the run

Between 1962 and 1964, 13 single women between the ages of 19 and 85 were murdered in the area of Boston, Massachusetts. Most were sexually assaulted and strangled in their own homes.

The lack of any signs of forced entry to properties suggested the killer was posing as a tradesman or official in order to gain access, and lone women were warned not to admit strangers into their homes.

The police investigation was hampered by the wide area of the killings, and problems occurred when a psychological profiler working for the police was discredited. A description of an assailant was given by one woman who survived an attack and eventually 33 year old former military policeman Albert de Salvo was charged after confessing and revealing details of the crimes to the police that had not been made public.

He was sentenced to life imprisonment but in February 1967 he escaped from Bridgewater State Hospital. A full scale manhunt ensued and he turned himself in three days later. Although he escaped the death penalty, his luck did not last: he was stabbed to death in prison in 1973 and his killers, presumably fellow inmates, were never identified.

Let it snow...let it snow...let it snow

Blizzard shuts down Chicago

Residents of Chicago, the 'windy city', were lulled into a false sense of security on Tuesday 24 January 1967, with unseasonably warm temperatures of 65F (18C). Weather forecasters predicted a 50% chance of moderate snowfalls of up to four inches.

All that changed on the morning of Thursday 26 January when snow began falling on the city and surrounding areas around 5 am. By 10 am, 23 inches (58.5cm) of snow had fallen.

Thousands were trapped in workplaces and schools, and on buses and trains which had become stranded. High winds added to the problems, driving huge snowdrifts across the city and closing Midway and O'Hare airports.

Despite help arriving from Iowa, Wisconsin and Michigan authorities, Mayor Richard J Daley asked the public to assist the city's workers in clearing the snow but by Friday, Chicago was virtually at a standstill.

Fortunately by the following Monday the snow stopped and the city began to return to normal. 26 people died as a result of the storm, which remains the worst on record.

Disaster on the launchpad

Crew killed as Apollo 1 rocket catches fire

America's mission to put a man on the moon by 1969 received a staggering blow when the crew of test rocket Apollo 1 were killed on 27 January 1967. Crew members Virgil Grissom, Edward White and Roger Chafee died when a fire broke out in the cabin of the rocket during a launch rehearsal at Cape Canaveral, Florida.

A series of mishaps caused the disaster: an electrical fault started the blaze which spread rapidly due to high oxygen levels and flammable materials in the cabin. Rescuers were generally unprepared: in particular, they were unable to open the cabin door due to pressure differences.

The tragedy led to a congressional investigation and the publication of the Phillips Report into safety at NASA. Manned Apollo flights were suspended for 20 months while the safety problems were addressed, and the first successful manned Apollo mission was flown in October 1968, followed by a successful moon landing in July 1969.

The crew of the ill-fated Apollo 1 mission.

Purple Haze
A song that defined a decade

On 17 March 1967 one of the defining songs of the sixties was released: *Purple Haze* by the Jimi Hendrix Experience. The group's second single, it featured a psychedelic sound with intensive guitar playing and the signature 'Hendrix chord' (E7♯9). The song began life when Hendrix was playing around with guitar riffs and his producer, Chas Chandler, overheard him. 'I heard him playing it at the flat and was knocked out. I told him to keep working on that, saying "that's the next single!"'

Hendrix wrote the rest of the song in his dressing room in London before a concert in December 1966. It was recorded in January 1967 at De Lane Lea Studios in London. Acoustical engineer Roger Mayer used some novel techniques in the recording to come up with a fresh sound that helped make the song a hit.

In the United Kingdom, *Purple Haze* spent fourteen weeks in the charts, peaking at number three. Hendrix and the band played it at several seminal 1960s concerts, including Monterey, Berkeley and Woodstock.

In 2005, *Q* Magazine rated the song as the greatest guitar track of all time.

Ryan goes to the gallows

The last man to be hanged in Australia

'God bless you – please make it quick'. Those were the last words of convicted killer Ronald Ryan to the hangman just before he became the last person to be executed in Australia, on 3 February 1967.

Career criminal Ryan, born in 1925, shot and killed unarmed prison warder John Hodson and seriously injured the prison chaplain during a daring escape from HM Prison Pentridge in Melbourne in December 1965. After several days on the run, a heavily armed Ryan was arrested before he was able to carry out his plan of fleeing to Brazil.

The trial caused a sensation in Australia and there were many objections to the passing of the death sentence. Australian law stated that a death by violence during a prison escape, even if not intentional, would be treated as murder, but it was not clear whether this applied outside the prison itself.

Despite widespread protests and a final appeal to the Queen for clemency, Ryan was hanged and buried in Pentridge.

In a final macabre twist, in 2007 his remains were exhumed and cremated after Hodson's daughter, while visiting the prison, jumped and danced on Ryan's grave. The death penalty in Australia was abolished in 1985.

Operation Junction City

The largest airborne assault since WWII

Operation Junction City was an 82-day military operation in the Vietnam War conducted by United States and south Vietnamese forces which started on 22 February 1967. It was the largest US airborne operation since 1945 and the only major airborne operation of the Vietnam War, and one of the largest U.S. operations of the war. It was named after Junction City, Kansas, home of the operation's commanding officer.

The aim of the operation was to locate and destroy the headquarters of the Viet Cong communist uprising in south Vietnam. A 'hammer and anvil' tactic was employed whereby ground troops would flush out the enemy who would then be trapped by the airborne forces.

Following the operation an estimated 2,728 Viet Cong soldiers were killed, with 300 American fatalities. The expected large headquarters was never found; it appeared that Viet Cong troops were more mobile and scattered than previously thought, with several high ranking officers having retreated to Cambodia.

Do be do be do!

Strangers in the Night wins Grammy Award

1967 saw crooner Frank Sinatra receive some coveted awards for his hit single of the previous year, *Strangers in the Night,* written by Bert Kaempfert, Charles Singleton and Eddie Snyder.

Sinatra received the Grammy Award for Best Male Pop Vocal Performance and Record of the Year award, with arranger Ernie Freeman receiving Best Arrangement. The single reached number one in both the US and UK. Since the 1960s it has become a 'standard' with several well known cover versions. Controversially, in 1967 French composer Michel Philippe-Gerard claimed the song had copied the tune of his 1953 composition *Magic Tango*, but the claim was thrown out by the courts in 1971.

Rumour has it that Sinatra sang his famous phrase 'do be do be do' in the song because he had forgotten the words – this seems rather unlikely, since this appears on the original studio recording!

Puppet on a String

Sandie Shaw wins Eurovision Song Contest

Today's Eurovision Song Contest may be considered a bit of a joke by some, but in 1967 it was a serious matter of national pride!

Popular singer Sandie Shaw entered the contest after being persuaded to take part by fellow pop singer Adam Faith, and her song *Puppet on a String* was chosen to represent the United Kingdom at the 1967 contest in Vienna to find the best song from the countries in the European Broadcasting Union.

Puppet on a String had one of the biggest victories in the competition's history – it received more than twice as many points as the second best song.

Despite the song reaching number one in the UK and topping charts worldwide, Sandie Shaw is said to have disliked it. Its writers, Bill Martin and Phil Coulter went on to have another success with *Congratulations* sung by Cliff Richard, which came second in the 1968 contest.

Sandie Shaw

Surveyor 3 bounces back

Lunar probe survives bumpy landing

Surveyor 3 was found by astronauts two years after its arrival in 1967.

Surveyor 3 was the third craft in NASA's Surveyor programme sent to explore the surface of the moon. Launched on 17 April 1967, the lander took three days to reach its destination.

Disaster almost struck when its engines failed to cut out close to the lunar surface, which caused the lander to hit the moon harder than planned. It bounced three times but eventually was able to land correctly without damage. The probe sent back thousands of TV images to earth and took soil samples which were then photographed and the images beamed back to NASA scientists.

During the first lunar night fourteen earth days after its landing, *Surveyor 3* succumbed to the extreme low temperatures on the moon's surface and ceased to function. When astronauts from Apollo 12 arrived on the moon in November 1969, they were able to find the probe and return parts of it to earth. It reamins the only probe visited by humans on another world.

Elizabeth Taylor wins Oscar

Award for *Who's Afraid of Virginia Woolf?*

Elizabeth Taylor (1932-2011) won her second Oscar for Best Actress, in the Academy Awards held on 10 April 1967.

Taylor's award was for her performance in the 1966 film *Who's Afraid of Virginia Woolf* directed by Mike Nichols and co-starring Taylor's real life husband Richard Burton.

The film itself was nominated for thirteen Academy Awards, and is one of only two films in its history to be nominated in every eligible category.

Taylor played Martha, a middle aged woman in a volatile marriage to an academic, unable to confront a secret from her past. Taylor gained 30 pounds to play the part.

The film lost out to *A Man for All Seasons* in the Best Picture category.

Military coup in Greece

The Colonels take over

Leaders of the junta

In the early hours of 21 April 1967, tanks appeared in strategic positions in the Greek capital, Athens. Troops rounded up leading politicians and by 6 am the prime minister, Panagiotis Kanellopolous, had been arrested.

Coup leader Brig-Gen Pattakos declared martial law and the suspension of the country's constitution with the consent of the King, who later claimed he had hoped to buy time to organise a counter-coup. This he attempted in December of that year, but the attempt failed and he was sent into exile.

The regime of the Colonels, which they claimed was a 'revolution to save the nation' from communism, lasted until 1973. The conspirators were sentenced to death, later commuted to life imprisonment.

King Constantine remained in exile in London until 2013, when he finally returned to his homeland.

Left: poster commemorating the coup

India's first Muslim president
Zakir Husain elected

On 13 May 1967 Zakir Husain (1897-1969) became the first Muslim president in predominantly Hindu India. He was also the shortest serving president and the first to die in office.

A prominent figure in India's movement for independence from Britain, Husain helped found the National Muslim University in 1920. His political career included serving as Governor of Bihar and the second vice president of India from 1962 to 1967. During his presidential tenure he led state visits to Hungary, Yugoslavia, the USSR and Nepal.

Lone yachtsman circles the globe

Sir Francis Chicester and *Gypsy Moth IV*

Commemorative medallion for Sir Francis Chichester

On 28 May 1967, British yachtsman and former RAF pilot Sir Francis Chichester (1901-1972) arrived in Plymouth, England, after an exhausting 226 day solo trip around the world in a 53' (16m) boat, *Gypsy Moth IV*, stopping only once, in Sydney, Australia.

This incredible achievement broke several records: fastest trip around the world by a small boat; twice the distance of any previous solo voyage, and the record speed for a singlehanded craft (1,400 miles in 8 days). Remarkably, Chichester was 66 years old and was in remission from a diagnosis of terminal lung cancer, but despite this was able to cope with terrific storms, broken steering and flooding.

In July 1967, Chichester was knighted by HM Queen Elizabeth II, using the same sword used by Elizabeth I to knight Sir Francis Drake, the first Englishman to sail around the world in a crewed ship almost 400 years earlier.

The Six Day War

Israel and Egypt clash in the Middle East

Between 5 and 10 June 1967, a short but bitter conflict took place between Israel and surrounding arab states, most notably Egypt, following border tensions which had grown since the establishment of the Jewish state of Israel in 1948.

Egypt's forces were led by General Nasser, famous from the 1956 Suez crisis, and a notable commander in Israel was Major-General Ariel Sharon, who went on to become Israel's prime minister. Expecting an attack, Israel responded pre-emptively and Egypt's air force was wiped out very quickly. Israel seized control of the Gaza Strip, Sinai Peninsula, West Bank and East Jerusalem, as well as the strategically important port of Sharm el Sheikh.

Although short, the war had long term effects: thousands of arab refugees left Israel, and Jews were expelled from countries across the arab world.

Israeli gunboat patrol near Sharm el Sheikh

Israel Government Press Office

Bond is back!

You Only Live Twice

Sean Connery returned as secret agent James Bond 007 in *You Only Live Twice*, the fifth film in the James Bond series, which premiered on 12 June 1967.

Bond is sent to Japan after the mysterious disappearance of American and Soviet spacecraft in orbit, where he tracks down the criminal mastermind behind the plot, arch-villain Ernst Stavros Blofeld, in a secret base beneath a volcano. Bond manages to destroy the base but Blofeld escapes.

The title of the film refers to Bond faking his own death in Hong Kong to avoid detection. Other notable scenes include the transformation of Bond – using a wig and makeup – into a Japanese fisherman, a disguise that is not altogether convincing!

The film was a smash hit which received positive reviews and grossed over $111 million worldwide.

During the filming it was announced that it was to be Connery's last outing in the role, although he was persuaded to return in two further films, *Diamonds are Forever* (1971) and *Never Say Never Again* (1983).

Mariner V visits Venus

Probe ends hopes that the Green Planet might support life

Venus, the green planet second from the sun, has always been shrouded in mystery, due to the constant heavy cloud layer hiding its surface from the view of telescopes on earth.

On 14 June 1967, NASA launched the Mariner 5 probe as part of its programme to explore the Venusian atmosphere. By 19 October the probe was able to fly by the planet and take measurements of temperature, pressure and other surface data. It was revealed that Venus had a far hotter surface and denser atmosphere than was previously thought, disappointing those that speculated it might be capable of supporting human life.

By November, the probe finished its operations. Although attempts to communicate with it were made in 1968 they did not meet with success, and it remains in a defunct orbit around the sun.

The Summer of Love

Monterey Festival marks the beginning of the hippy era

A protestor offers flowers to military police during an anti-Vietnam war protest.

The 1960s is known as the era of 'flower power' and hippies. The earlier part of the decade had more in common with the strait-laced 1950s but by 1967 the sub-culture of the 'flower children', descendants of the earlier 'beatniks', had begun to flourish, particularly in the San Francisco area of California.

As one undergraduate of the time observed, at the end of the spring term he left university in a tweed jacket and tie. In the autumn term, he returned in a kaftan and beads! The movement was popular with middle class young people and focused on psychedelic music and art, mind expanding drugs and left-wing politics.

This culminated with the social phenomenon known as the Summer of Love, a term coined by a group of young people in the Haight-Ashbury area of San Franciso. Although a number of events took place, the starting point was probably the Monterey Festival in California in June. This was hugely popular with bands such as The Who, Grateful Dead and the Jimi Hendrix Experience attending.

'I ain't got no quarrel with them Viet Cong'

Muhammed Ali refuses to serve in US Army

Legendary boxer Muhammed Ali was called up for military service in April 1967. (Conscription – 'the draft' – was enforced in the USA from 1940 to 1973). As a Muslim convert, Ali declared himself to be a conscientious objector, saying 'I ain't got no quarrel with them Viet Cong'. He was arrested and stripped of his boxing licence and title by the New York State Athletic Commission, a ban which was to last three years.

At his trial on 20 June he was found guilty of draft evasion, but the case was referred to the Supreme Court and Ali remained free until its decision was made in 1971, when it was ruled that Ali should have been exempted on grounds of conscience.

During the run up to the trial, Ali travelled widely, speaking at universities and colleges as part of the growing movement of opposition to the Vietnam war.

Muhammed Ali

A 'chocolate machine for cash'

The world's first ATM opens

Barclay's Bank in Enfield, London: site of the world's first ATM

A strange new sight appeared on the suburban high street of Enfield, north London on 27 June 1967: a 'hole in the wall' outside Barclay's Bank which dispensed bank notes. A familar concept today, it was a completely novel idea when it was declared open by popular British comedy actor Reg Varney, star of TV series *On the Buses*.

Although other prototypes had been patented in the early 1960s, the De La Rue machine in Enfield created by engineer John Shepherd-Barron, who was inspired by a chocolate bar dispenser, is generally acknowledged to be the world's first.

Rather than a plastic card, customers used carbon-marked paper slips. Shortly afterwards, the machine was followed by others including the Bankomat in Sweden and the Chubb MD2 in England. The USA had to wait until 1969 when the first ATM was installed at the Chemical Bank in New York.

BBC broadcasts in colour

Wimbledon tennis match is the first programme

Although colour television had been available in the USA since the 1950s, it was not until 1967 that British viewers were able to watch broadcasts in 'living colour.'

The first colour programme to be transmitted, on BBC2 on 1 July 1967 was coverage of the Wimbledon tennis championships. Gradually the number of colour programmes increased, with BBC1 and ITV beginning colour programming in 1969, including notable broadcasts suited to the medium such as the investiture of Prince Charles as Prince of Wales, and Kenneth Clark's series on the history of art, *Civilization*. By 1970 all parts of the UK were able to receive colour programmes. A colour licence cost £10 per year, twice the cost of that for a black and white set.

Colour television spread throughout Europe and the rest of the world in the 1970s, with Cambodia being the last country to begin broadcasting, in 1985.

A technician demonstrates colour TV.

Sexual Offences Act

Homosexual acts decriminalised

Leo Abse MP proposed legislation to decriminalise homosexual acts

Homosexual activity between men had been legislated against in England and Wales since the sixteenth century, and from the 1880s began to be more widely restricted.

By the 1950s, a relaxation of public opinion and concern over the law being a 'blackmailer's charter' against homosexuals in positions of authority, led to a review of the legislation in the a report by the Wolfenden Committee, a panel which included academics, doctors and clergy.

In 1965 politicians Leo Abse MP and Lord Arran drew heavily on the committee's proposals in their Sexual Offences Bill which received royal assent on 27 July 1967.

The Act legalised consenting homosexual acts in private between men aged over 21 (women were never subject to legislation) but did not include men serving in the armed forces or merchant navy. Scotland enacted similar legislation in 1980 and Northern Ireland in 1982.

The Biafran War

Conflict leads to famine in Nigeria

Nigeria saw the outbreak of over two years of bitter civil war on 6 July 1967. Unrest had been simmering since the country became independent from Britain in 1960. On 30 May 1967 the mainly Christian Igbo tribe led the secession of the breakaway state of Biafra in the southern part of the country from the predominantly Muslim north.

Within a year, the federal government of Nigeria had surrounded Biafra and seized the important oil facilities at Port Harcourt.

Severe famine ensued, with between half a million and two million Biafrans thought to have died from starvation.

The famine caught the attention of the world's media, with pictures of starving Biafrans appearing on television and in newspapers. This led to a rise in prominence of many famine relief organisations such as *Médecins Sans Frontières*.

In 1969 the federal forces launched a final offensive and on 14 January 1970 Biafra formally surrendered.

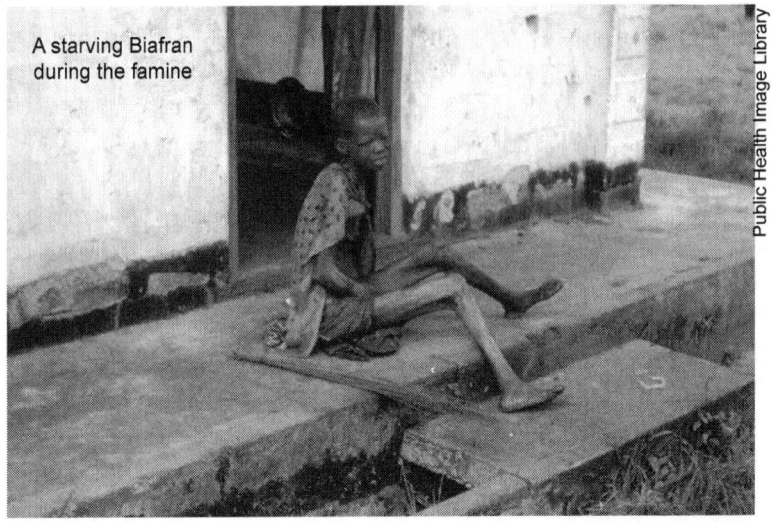

A starving Biafran during the famine

Public Health Image Library

Vive le Québec libre!

De Gaulle makes controversial speech

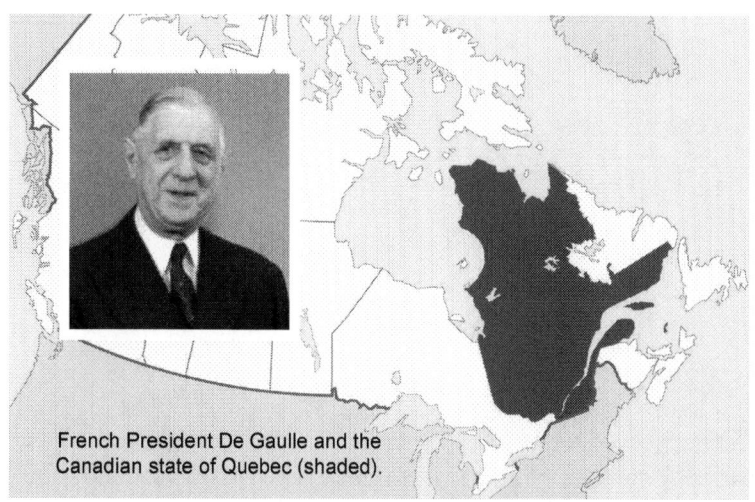

French President De Gaulle and the Canadian state of Quebec (shaded).

On 24 July 1967 French President Charles De Gaulle, whilst on an official visit to Canada, made a controversial speech to a large crowd at Montreal City Hall which was to be a turning point in Franco-Canadian relations. During the speech he said '*Vive Montréal; Vive le Québec!*' ('Long live Montreal, Long live Quebec!'). He then followed this with *'Vive le Québec libre!'* ('Long live free Quebec!')

French-speaking Quebec, originally a French colony but under British control from 1774, had a strong independence movement and this speech was seen as an endorsement of it. De Gaulle's speech was criticised by the media, both in France and Canada, and he cut short his visit, with the Canadian prime minister, Lester B Pearson saying that 'Canadians do not need to be liberated.'

Despite De Gaulle's boost to the independence movement, Quebec voted against independence in referenda in 1980 and 1995.

Scuppering the pirates

Britain bans 'pirate radio'

Pirate radio ship Caroline. DJs included Emperor Rothko (right)

Until 1973, the BBC had a legal monopoly on radio broadcasting based in the United Kingdom. This meant any commercial stations had to be based overseas, such as Radio Luxembourg, which started in the 1930s. Difficulties in broadcasting from such a distance led to the development of 'pirate radio' – stations based on ships moored off the coast.

Stations such as Radio Caroline flourished as British listeners used to the more staid style of BBC broadcasts could now hear an upbeat (and some might say down-market) mixture of pop music and informal chat, with many presenters, such as Tony Blackburn, going on to become famous names on the BBC. In an attempt to clamp down on unofficial broadcasting, the Marine &c, Broadcasting (Offences) Act became law on 14 August 1967. This made it illegal for offshore radio stations to employ British citizens.

Attempts were made to get round this, but proved largely impractical. The pirates limped along until further legislation finished them off for good in 1990, but by that time their listeners had largely retuned to the new BBC radio stations 1 and 2, with a style based on that of the pirates and which employed many former pirate presenters themselves.

Ceausescu in charge

Hardline leader takes over in Romania

Nicolae Ceausescu (1918-1918) was born in poverty in the eastern European country of Romania. As a young man he joined the Communist Party. When the country fell to the Communists following the second world war, Ceausescu's political career enjoyed a rapid rise.

By the 1950s he held the second highest position in the party and when President Gheorghiu-Dej died in 1965, Ceausescu took over. In 1967, he took complete control of the country. Popular at first particularly with western governments who saw him as a moderate, he gradually drove the country to ruin with his totalitarian policies and desperate attempts at industrialisation. His social reforms failed also: a repopulation programme backfired, with large numbers of unwanted babies abandoned in state orphanages.

By 1989, Romanians had had enough, and nationwide demonstrations against him erupted into revolution. He was captured and tried by a revolutionary council, and he and his wife Elena were executed by firing squad on Christmas Day, 1989.

Sealand for ever!

The world's smallest 'country' is declared

On 2 September 1967, eccentric Englishman Major Paddy Roy Bates, a former pirate radio disc jockey, declared himself Prince of the world's smallest state – The Principality of Sealand. His 'country' was a rusting iron platform in the North Sea, a second world war defensive platform known as a Maunsell Fort.

Bates was arrested after his son fired shots at a Royal Navy ship near the platform. The court threw out the case because it took place outside British territorial waters. Bates took this as recognition of his country and issued a constitution, flag, passports, currency and national anthem.

Although not recognised as a country by any other, in 1978 Germany sent a diplomat to Sealand to negotiate after a German, Alexander Achenbach tried to take over the platform. Despite Bates' belief that the diplomatic mission added further legitimacy to his claim to statehood, the United Nations never recognised it, and since 1987 the platform has lain with UK territorial waters.

Bates died in 2012 but his son, 'Prince Michael' took over and Sealand has since boasted a football team and an internet hosting facility. Alexander Achenbach continues to pursue his claim and heads the 'Sealand Rebel Government' in Germany!

The former WW2 gun platform: now the Principality of Sealand.

Sweden changes sides

Drivers move from left to right

Stockholm traffic in confusion

Dagen H (H Day), was the code-name for 3 September 1967, when Swedish drivers were required to change from the left to the right hand side of the road to bring the traffic network in line with neighbouring countries.

Plans for this monumental undertaking had been underway since 1963, despite the population voting against the change when previously proposed in 1955.

The government prepared new road signs and markings and issued items to help people remember, such as driving gloves marked with 'left' and 'right', and even commissioned a pop song, *Keep to the Right, Svensson* by The Telstars.

Dagen H took place on a Sunday; all non-essential traffic was banned between 01.00 and 06.00. Any vehicles still on the road had to come to a complete halt at 04.50 then change sides and stop again until proceeding with caution at 05.00. In major cities the changeover took longer, with bans in place until the afternoon.

The orderly Swedes managed to get through the day relatively unscathed; in fact accident levels dipped until 1969, probably due to increased caution by drivers.

Rock steady

Gibraltar votes to remain British

The tiny peninsula of Gibraltar with its quaint English houses and famous towering rock, at the southern tip of Spain, was ceded to Britain in perpetuity by the Spanish following the Treaty of Utrecht in 1713. The colony became an important military base which controlled the passage of shipping through the western Mediterranean.

With the advent of air travel this became less important and by the 1960s, the Spanish government made formal proposals to return Gibraltar to Spanish control. At the time Spain was under the control of dictator General Franco and poverty levels were high on the frontier; unsuprisingly in the referendum held on 10 September, 99% of Gibraltarians voted to remain British.

Following the referendum, Ango-Spanish relations broke down somewhat, and the Gibraltarian-Spanish border was closed in 1969, not to reopen until 1985.

A Gibraltarian car painted in British colours

'I name this ship...myself'

Queen Elizabeth II launches *Queen Elizabeth II*

By the mid 1960s, air travel had become the most popular means of crossing the Atlantic. Ocean liners such as the *Queen Mary* and *Queen Elizabeth* were increasingly out-dated and uneconomical. Ship builder Cunard decide to gamble on a slimmed down, modernised liner, the *Queen Elizabeth II*.

Work began in 1965 at the John Brown Shipyard in Clydebank near Glasgow. On 20 September 1967 she was named and launched by her namesake, Queen Elizabeth II, using the same pair of gold scissors her mother and grandmother used to launch the *Queen Elizabeth* and *Queen Mary* respectively. Her first cruise was to Las Palmas in April 1969.

The ship utilised the latest technology to be able to cruise at 28.5 knots (52.8km/h) using half the fuel of earlier liners. A shallower draught meant the ship could visit ports that the old liners had been unable to.

QE2 went on to give many years of service, including a stint as a troopship during the Falklands War. She was retired from service in 2007 and now lies mothballed in Dubai.

'I am not a number!'

Cult series *The Prisoner* first broadcast

Number Six (Patrick McGoohan, inset) was held captive in a mysterious village, filmed at Portmeirion in Wales.

Cult TV series *The Prisoner*, starring Patrick MacGoohan, was first broadcast in September 1967. The series follows a former British secret agent who is kidnapped and taken to a mysterious remote village, from which it is impossible to escape.

The agent, known only as Number Six, attempts to find out why he is being held and what side the village authorities are working for. A cat and mouse game ensues between Number Six and his captors, with all the paraphenalia of sixties spy thrillers involved: mind control, hallucinogenics and dream manipulation.

By the end of the series it was never really clear what it was all about – perhaps one of the reasons why it became a cult.

A change of stations
BBC relaunches its radio service

BBC radio in the UK had for many years been divided into the Home Service (news, current affairs and religious broadcasting), the Third Programme (classical music and culture) and the Light Programme (popular music, sport and entertainment).

Changing public tastes and competition from pirate radio stations led to a review of the setup, and on 30 September 1967 BBC radio was relaunched with the Home Service renamed Radio Four, the Third Programme, Radio Three, and the Light Programme split into Radio Two and Radio One. The first song played on Radio One was *Flowers in the Rain* by The Move, on a programme presented by DJ Tony Blackburn, already familiar to listeners from his time on Radio Caroline.

Although the new Radio One was popular, with audiences reaching 20 million for some shows in the 1970s, some musicians still felt it was too 'establishment', with Joe Strummer saying 'there's no radio station for young people anymore.'

The Move, whose song *Flowers in the Rain* was the first record played on the BBC's new station, Radio One.

Che Guevara killed

Argentinian revolutionary shot dead

Ernesto 'Che' Guevara, born 1928, initially qualified as a doctor but went on to become a marxist revolutionary and a sixties icon.

After meeting Fidel Castro he became an insurgent with him in Cuba, fighting against the Batista government. Following the Cuban revolution, Guevara played a key role in the new government.

In 1965 he left to foment revolution abroad, firstly in the Congo and then in Bolivia where he raised the National Liberation Army. The revolution did not transpire as he had hoped, and he was eventually captured and summarily executed by Bolivian soldiers on 9 October 1967.

Fidel Castro declared three days of mourning in Cuba and Guevara's legendary status among 1960s radicals was assured. His legacy, however, remains contentious, with some commentators describing him as a cold-blooded killer and fanatic.

Emergency in Aden

British withdraw from troubled colony

The central location of the city of Aden in the gulf of Arabia, on the sea routes between India, Africa and Britain made it a desirable spot for ships to refuel at its oil refinery and take on supplies during the long trip to India when it was under British rule.

After Indian independence in 1947 its importance to Britain dwindled, and by the 1960s the city, and its hinterland (known as the Aden Protectorate) were under attack from communist insurgents. Britain announced plans for independence in 1964, but by 1967 the situation had deteriorated rapidly, with widespread rioting and attacks on British families.

By 13 December 1967 all British civilians and military had been evacuated, following the declaration of the People's Republic of South Yemen on 30 November. The area remains a troublespot to this day.

British troops patrolling the streets of Aden.

The heart of the matter

Miracle doctor performs first human heart transplant

Dr Barnard at a press conference

Although a heart transplant had been performed in 1964 by Dr James D Hardy using a chimpanzee's heart, the patient died within an hour without regaining consciousness.

The first human heart transplant was not attempted until 3 December 1967, when Dr Christiaan Barnard (1922-2001) transplanted the heart of a recently deceased accident victim into 54 year old Louis Washkansky at a hospital in Cape Town, South Africa. Due to a weakened immune system, Mr Washkansky died 18 days later, but Barnard had proved the transplantation itself could be a success.

In 1968, the recipient of Dr Barnard's second transplant lived for 19 months and by the 1970s the surgery had become widespread, with survival rates measured in years rather than months.

Sullivan slams The Doors

Band barred from *Ed Sullivan Show*

The Doors, led by James Douglas 'Jim' Morrison (1943-1971), remain one of the decade's iconic rock bands.

In the summer of 1967 their single *Light my Fire* spent three weeks at number one in the US charts, a meteoric rise for a group who had the same year been playing in high schools and warm-up acts.

The group were invited to play *Light my Fire* on the popular Ed Sullivan TV show, but the show's producers insisted that Morrison change the lyrics of the song to remove a perceived drugs reference. The band agreed but while live on air changed their mind and sang the original lyrics.

Sullivan refused to shake hands with the band and barred them from appearing on his show again. Their status as rock rebels was thereafter assured, but Morrison went into decline and was eventually found dead, probably of natural causes, in an apartment in Paris in 1971.

Jim Morrison of The Doors.
Inset: Ed Sullivan

Tragedy on the Ohio River

46 killed as Silver Bridge collapses

Disaster struck the states of Ohio and West Virginia on 15 December 1967. The Silver Bridge, which carried US Route 35 over the Ohio River, collapsed completely in little more than a minute during rush hour.

46 people died. Following investigations it was found that a tiny defect just 0.1 inches deep on part of a suspension chain had caused the collapse.

The bridge, built in 1928, had been carrying far heavier loads than it had been designed for – the average car being much heavier in 1967 than in 1928.

Following the disaster, a similarly constructed bridge upstream at St Mary's, West Virginia, was immediately closed. The collapse lead to legislation to ensure older bridges in the US were better maintained.

Australian PM disappears

Harold Holt presumed drowned

The mystery of the disappearing Australian Prime Minister, Harold Holt, has never been solved. On the morning of 17 December 1967, Holt went swimming at Cheviot Beach near Portsea in Victoria, Australia.

After disappearing from view, friends on the beach raised the alarm, but despite an extensive search by the police, Royal Australian Navy and Air Force and local volunteers no trace of his body was found.

Two days later, the government officially announced that Holt was believed drowned. Deputy Prime Minister John McEwen was sworn in until an election could be held.

A memorial service was held at St Paul's Cathedral in Melbourne on 22 December, attended by US President Lydon Johnson, Prince Charles and British Prime Minister Harold Wilson.

Holt was a strong swimmer, but had been suffering from ill health and had twice been taken ill while swimming that year. Despite this, conspiracy theories circulated, with suggestions of suicide and even abduction by Chinese secret agents.

Somewhat ironically, Holt's lasting memorial is the Harold Holt Swimming Centre in Melbourne, named in his honour.

Cheviot Beach with (inset) Harold Holt.

Robyn Cox/National Archives of Australia

A fab year for the Fab Four

Films, albums and multiple hits

1967 was the year of peak output for the Beatles. They released their most famous album, the psychedelia-influenced *Sergeant Pepper's Lonely Hearts Club Band,* as well as the single *Strawberry Fields Forever* with the 'double A' side of *Penny Lane*.

Later in the year the film and associated album *Magical Mystery Tour* came out, which included the hit song *All You Need is Love*. This was performed by the band in the world's first live global TV broadcast on 25 June 1967, watched by over 400 million people. The song itself reached number one in most countries around the globe. The single *Hello Goodbye* also shot to number one. During the year the band also wrote and recorded most of the material for their forthcoming animated film *Yellow Submarine*.

Despite it being the peak of the band's career, it was also marred by tragedy – manager Brian Epstein died of a drugs overdose, aged just 32. Despite further hits, films and albums, the band never bettered their achievements of 1967, and finally split in 1970.

Parlophone Music Sweden

BIRTHDAY NOTEBOOKS

FROM
MONTPELIER PUBLISHING

Handy 60-page ruled notebooks with a significant event of the year on each page.

A great alternative to a birthday card.
Available from Amazon.

Printed in Great Britain
by Amazon